Steps to Success

DIGRAPHS

A Step by Step Guide for Using Digraphs to Improve Your Listening, Writing, and Pronunciation Skills.

By

Cesar Carrasco, M.Ed.

All rights reserved.

This workbook or parts thereof may not be reproduced or transmitted in any form, including electronic, photocopy recording, or storage of information, without written permission from the publisher.

ISBN: 978-1-7322579-9-3 (Paperback)

978-1-7322579-8-6 (Ebook)

Telephone: (951) 760-9718

Temecula, Ca.

About the Author

I would like to thank you for your interest in taking the first *Steps to Success* in learning a second language. My educational background consists of having a bachelor's and Master's Degree in Education, a teaching credential, and a credential in Special Education. I began my career in the educational field in 1991 and since then, I have taught Kindergarten through 12th grade, Adult Education in the areas of English as Second Language (ESL) and High School subjects, and helped high school students and adults to obtain their high school diploma. I am currently an elementary principal and I have 18 years experience in the administrative field. I continue to support high school students to obtain their high school diploma and continue assisting adults in refining and helping them with English Language Development through ESL classes. My extensive experience teaching English as a Second Language has enabled me to streamline teaching practices in the English Language.

My goal in *Steps to Success - DIGRAPHS* is to provide a basic method explaining and demonstrating how digraphs are made up and where they can be found in words. Students will have opportunities to listen to and watch Videos modeling digraph and word pronunciation. *Steps to Success - DIGRAPHS* is a basic method highlighting readiness skills in English Grammar and Usage. Skills are easy to understand and are translated to Spanish to support Listening and Writing comprehension. It is a comprehensive guide to strengthening conversational skills through listening, repeating words, and practicing oral language development through writing skills.

I am very confident that this will help you to build and strengthen your vocabulary skills and listening skills. If you are interested in pursuing this practice, you will receive Videos that will assist you with your pronunciation skills to become more successful in conversing with others. As you begin to work with this workbook, make sure that you take the Pre and Post Tests to set a benchmark that will show your progress as you work throughout this workbook. I am confident that the extensive amount of exercises that are shown in *Steps to Success - DIGRAPHS* will ensure that you build comprehensive English skills.

Acknowledgements

I would like to thank everyone who has supported my project starting with my wonderful wife, Keri, and my two children, Taylor and Kassidy. A huge thank you to my two brothers and sister-in-laws for their guidance and support. I also want to acknowledge Alma Wright, for her collaboration in providing the graphic design, technical support and producing our video collection. Mrs. Ingrid Weisentengar for her assistance in teaching the lessons provided in the video collection.

Cesar Carrasco, M.Ed.

Sobre el Autor

Me gustaría darles las gracias por su interés en tomar los primeros pasos hacia el éxito en aprender un Segundo idioma. Mi educación consiste de una Licenciatura en Educación y Maestría en Administración, credenciales en la enseñanza de Educación regular y enseñanza en Educación Especial. Mi carrera profesional comenzó en 1991 y desde este tiempo, mi enfoque ha sido en los grados de el kínder hasta el duodécimo grado, Escuela para Educación para Adultos en la destreza del idioma del inglés (English as a Second Language en Palomar College and Escuela de Adultos) y apoyando a estudiantes en la preparatoria abierta en obtener un certificado de preparatoria. Actualmente soy director de una escuela primaria y mi experiencia como administrador tiene una trayectoria de 18 años. Mi experiencia en la rama de inglés como segundo idioma me permite racionalizar la práctica de enseñanza para el idioma del inglés.

Mi meta en usar *"DIGRAPHS," Steps to Success*, es ofrecer un método básico que explica y demuestra como los dígrafos son compuestos y donde se pueden encontrar en las palabras. Los estudiantes tendrán oportunidades de escuchar y ver los Videos que muestran lo que es un dígrafo y su pronunciación. *Steps to Success – DIGRAPHS* es un método básico que ensena las destrezas del uso de la gramática en ingles usando vocabulario que representan los dígrafos. Los ejercicios son fáciles de entender y también son traducidos al español para apoyar la enseñanza de escuchar el vocabulario en inglés y la comprensión de la escritura. El volumen de Digraphs es una guía básica para fortalecer las destrezas de conversación usando la rutina de escuchar vocabulario, repetir el vocabulario que se está enseñando, y practicar el desarrollo oralmente usando estrategias de escritura.

Tengo la confianza de que este método, *Steps to Success - DIGRAPHS* le ayudara a crear y fortalecer el desarrollo de practicar vocabulario y la destreza de escuchar vocabulario para refinar la pronunciación. Si usted está dispuesto a enfrentar esta práctica, usted recibirá Videos que le ayudara con la pronunciación para tener éxito en conversar con los demás en el idioma inglés. Al comienzo de este método es importante de que usted tome el pre exámenes y los exámenes a la mitad y final del libro para tener una guía de su progreso de aprendizaje. También tengo la confianza que Steps to Success DIGRAPHS les proveerá una guía detallada para construir destrezas del idioma ingles con éxito usando el amplio volumen de ejercicios detallados y descriptivos.

Un Cordial Saludo,

Cesar Carrasco

TABLE OF CONTENTS

PURPOSE OF TAKING A PRETEST 5
- Pretest 7
- DIGRAPHS 9

DIGRAPHS 9
- Discriminating the /ch/ digraph 10
- Discriminating the /ph/ digraph 17

MORE DIGRAPHS 24
- Discriminating the /th/ digraph sound 24
- Discriminating the /sh/ digraph sound 27
- Discriminating the /kn/ digraph sound 31

SHARPENING YOUR WRITING SKILLS 33
- Rules to Follow when writing informational questions with /ch/ and /ph/ digraphs 33
- table showing pronouns and helping verbs 33
- Writing Exercises using the /ch/ digraph 34
- Writing Exercises using the /ph/ digraph 37

MAKING STATEMENTS USING "WHERE" 40
- Rules to Follow when Writing Informational Questions Using /sh/ and /wh/ Digraphs 40
- Table of Prepositions of Location 41

MAKING STATEMENTS WITH "WHERE" USING LINKING VERBS AND PREPOSITIONS 44
- Making Informational Questions with "where" that show no action using the /sh/ and /wh/ digraphs 44

MAKING STATEMENTS WITH "WHERE" AND "WHAT" AND ACTION WORDS 48
- Making informational Questions with "where" that show action using the /th/ and /kn/ digraphs 51

QUESTIONS WITH "WHY" AND ACTION WORDS 54

ADJECTIVES 56
- Describing Pictures with the /ch/, /th/, /kn/ digraphs 58

POST TEST 61

EXAMENES PRELIMINARES

Porque sería practico tomar los examenes preliminares.

El propósito de los examenes preliminares sirven para determinar el material que será necesario estudiar para el desarrollo del idioma Ingles. Los resultados de los examenes preliminares también te ayudaran a desarrollar un plan de estudio.

Los examenes preliminares consisten de preguntas basadas en el contexto del libro *Steps to Success, Digraphs.*

Tome el examen preliminar. Elija la mejor respuesta para cada pregunta. Recuerde que el objetivo de esta evaluación es para darnos una idea de las destrezas que se necesitan para desarrollar el idioma de Ingles.

PRETEST

Why should I take the Pretest?

The purpose of the pretest is to help you determine which skills you need to strengthen. The results of the pretest will assist you to arrange a unit of study to help you develop your English Language Development skills.

The pretest consists of multiple-choice and true or false questions. These questions are based on the content of the book *Steps to Success, Digraphs.*

As you begin to take the pretest, it is important for you to answer each question carefully. Choose the best answer. Remember, the objective of taking a pretest is to give you an idea of the skills you need to develop.

When you have completed the pretest, check your answers to begin planning your framework of study.

Steps to Success Digraph

Pretest

1. **Read each question and circle the best answer.**

    a. A digraph can be found in _____.

       a. the middle of a word.
       b. the beginning of a word.
       c. the beginning, middle, or end of a word.

    b. A digraph _____.

       a. is made up of two letters that are combined together to make a single sound.
       b. is made up of two letters to make two sounds.
       c. is made up of many letters, each making its own sound.
       d. none of the above.

2. **True or False: After you read each question, write True or False on the blank line to justify the statement.**

    c. _____ Digraphs are two consonants that can be articulated into one sound.

    d. _____ A digraph can be found either at the beginning or end of a word.

    e. _____ The purpose of working with digraph sounds is to understand that two letters work together to make a single sound.

3. Look at each set of pictures and circle the letter of the picture that makes the initial sound /ch/.

f.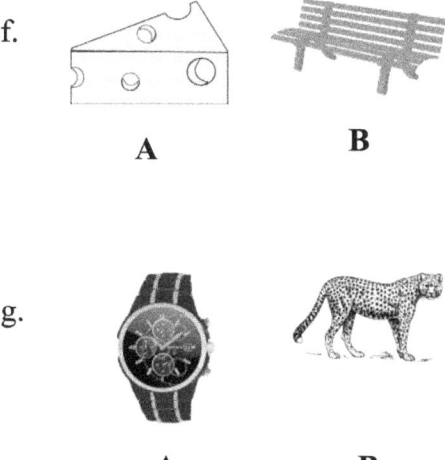
   A   B

g.
   A   B

4. Look at each set of pictures and circle the letter of the picture that makes the /ph/ sound in the middle of a word.

h.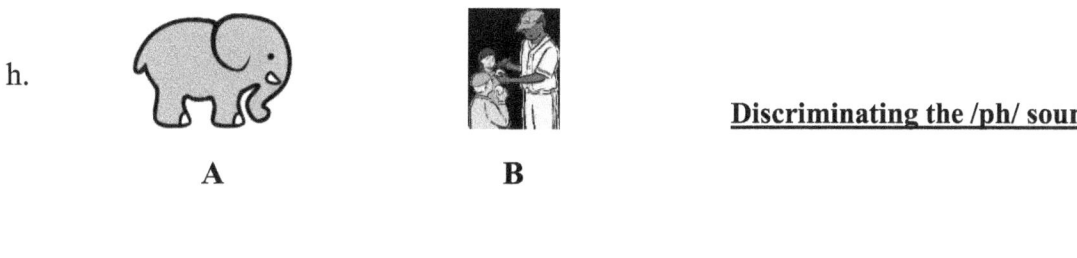
   A   B   **Discriminating the /ph/ sound**

i.
   A   B

j.
   A   B

DIGRAPHS

- A **digraph** is made of two letters that are combined together to make a single sound.

- A **digraph** can be found in the beginning, middle, or end of a word.

- The following combinations make up digraphs at the <u>beginning</u>, <u>middle</u>, or <u>end</u> of a word:

  | ch, | ph, | kn, | gh, | ng, | sh, | wh, | th |

- Digraphs are made up of consonants that articulate speech sounds using full or partial closure of our vocal tract. As you work towards completing each exercise in this *Volume, DIGRAPHS*, it is important for you to be aware that a digraph is made up of two consonants and together they make one sound.

- Throughout each section, you will have the opportunity to practice expressing vocabulary that contains digraphs. You will have access to visuals demonstrating how each of the following digraphs is articulated.

  | ch | ph | kn | gh | ng | sh | wh | th |

- The first exercise will focus on the /ch/ digraph and thereafter we will cover the rest of the digraphs in the order you see them. You will have an opportunity to work with each digraph in depth following similar drill routines with the goal for you to understand how two consonants are being articulated into one sound.

- **EXERCISE #1: Discriminating the /ch/ digraph sound.**

    Look at each word in the Word Bank list and practice saying the initial digraph in each word. (Use the QR to assist you in practicing the pronunciation)

    ## Word Bank

    Chain (noun) \chān\

    chalk (noun) \chăk\

    check (noun) \chêk\

    cheese (noun) \chēz\

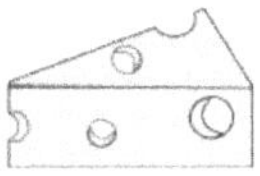

    chef (noun) \shef\

    chess (noun) \chês\

    chief (noun) \cheef\

    chimp (noun) \chimp\

    champion (noun) \chăm' pē-en\

    Chair (noun) \cher\

    chapel (noun) \chăp êl\

    cheek (noun) \chēk\

    cheetah (noun) \chee-tuh]

    cherry (noun) \cher-ee\

    chick (noun) \chĭk\

    child (noun) \chīld\

    chin (noun) \chĭn\

    channel (noun) \chanel\

    Follow and scan the QR code to view the tutorial video on this topic.
    Sigue y escanea el código QR para ver el video tutorial sobre este tema.

DIGRAFOS

- Dígrafos son compuestos de dos letras que son combinadas para hacer un sonido singular.

- Un dígrafo se puede encontrar al comienzo, en medio, o al final de una palabra.

- Las siguientes combinaciones componen dígrafos al principio de una palabra:

> **ch,   ph,   kn,   gh,   ng,   sh,   wh,   th**

- Dígrafos son compuestos de consonantes que expresan el sonido de habla usando toda o cierre parcial de nuestra vía vocal. Durante su trabajo en terminar cada ejercicio en el Volumen, Dígrafos, es importante de que este consciente de que un dígrafo es un sonido compuesto de dos letras que representan una fonema y se leen como una.

- En cada sección, tendrá la oportunidad de practicar expresando el vocabulario que contienen dígrafos. Tendrá acceso a demonstraciones visuales que modelan como expresar los siguientes dígrafos:

> **ch,   ph,   kn,   gh,   ng,   sh,   wh,   th**

- El primer ejercicio se enfocara en el dígrafo /ch/ y trabajaremos más a fondo para que pueda entender como dos consonantes se usan para hacer un solo sonido. Después, practicaras otros dígrafos en rutinas similares.

- **NOTAS:**

_____

_____

_____

- # EXERCISE #2: Discriminating the /ch/ sound.

Look at each set of pictures, listen to each word, then circle the correct picture that has the /ch/ digraph sound. (Use the QR to assist you in this next exercise)

1)  A B

2) 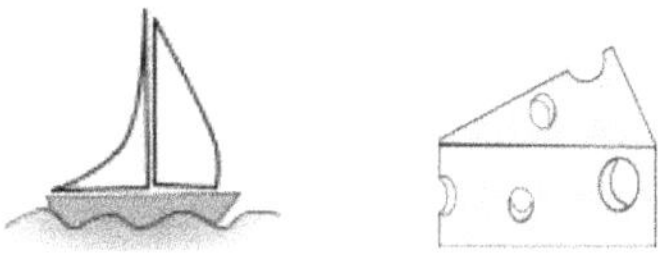 C D

3) 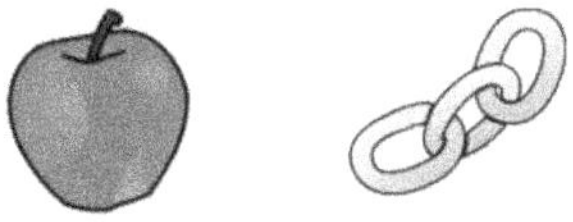 A B

4) 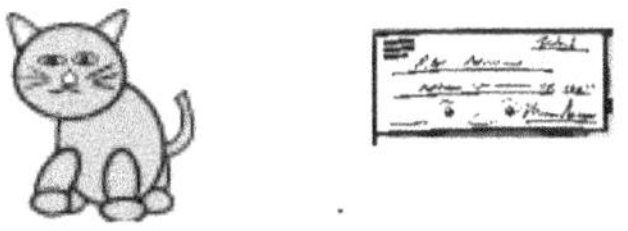 C D

5)  A B

6)  C D

7)  A B

8)  C D

Follow and scan the QR code to view the tutorial video on this topic.
Sigue y escanea el código QR para ver el video tutorial sobre este tema.

Steps to Success Digraph

 **Rule to remember: A digraph is made up of two consonants and together they make one sound.**

- ### Exercise #3:

The /ch/ digraph can also be found in the middle or the end of a word.

Look at the words on the list below and practice pronouncing each word (Use the QR to assist you in pronouncing the word). Make sure you emphasize the /ch/ sound.

Word Bank

church (n) \church\

peach (n) \pēch\

preacher (n) \prēch' er\

teacher (n) \teach' er\

beach (n) \bēch\

lunch (n) \lŭnch\

patch (n) \păch\

porch (n) \pōrch\

stitches (n) 'stĭches\

branch (n) \branch\

bench (n) \bench\

ditch (n) \dich\

12

sandwich (n)\ san wich\

couch (n) \kaŭch\

pouch (n) \paŭch\

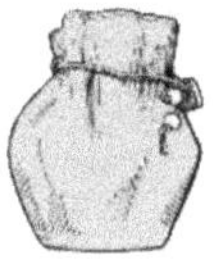

ranch (n) \ranch\

cockroach (n) \kok rōch\

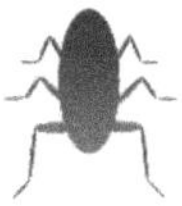

torch (n) \tōrch\

watch (n) \wăch\

butcher (n) \bŭ chŭr\

pitcher (n) \pĭ chŭr\

catcher (n) \ka chŭr\

kitchen (n) \kĭ chen\

crutch (n) \krŭch\

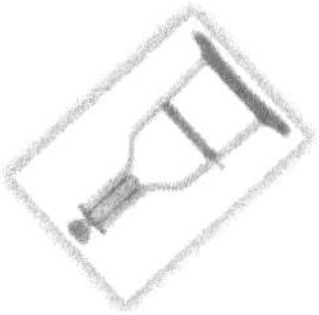

Follow and scan the QR code to view the tutorial video on this topic.
Sigue y escanea el código QR para ver el video tutorial sobre este tema.

NOTES:

_____

_____

- **EXERCISE #4: Discriminating the /ch/ sound at the beginning, middle, and end of a word.**

    Look at each set of pictures, listen to each word, and then circle the correct picture that makes the /ch/ digraph sound. (Use the QR to assist you in this next exercise)

1)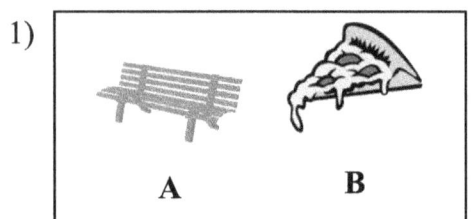

2)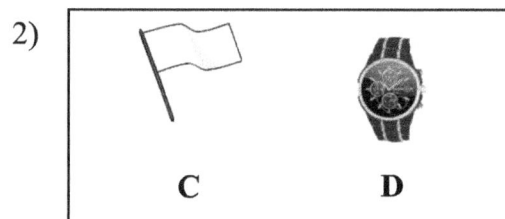

3)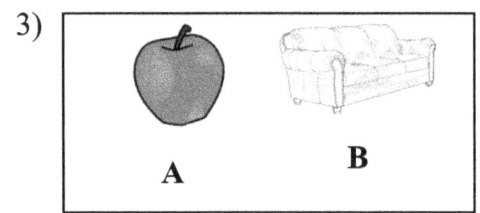

4)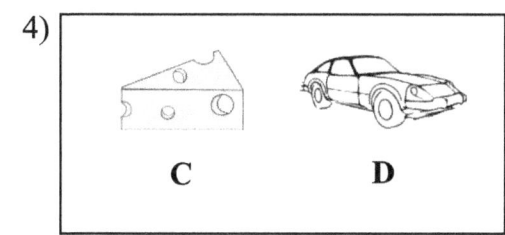

5)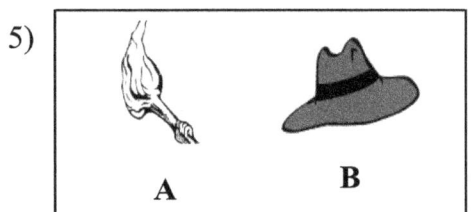

6)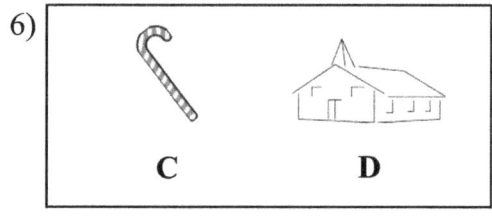

7)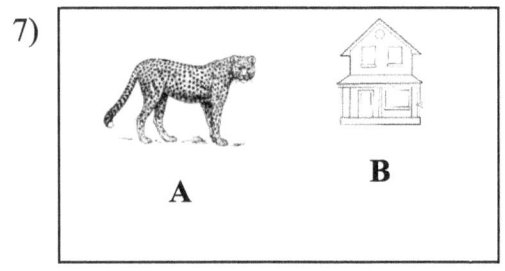

8)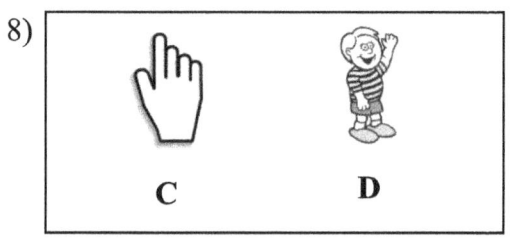

9)   A / B

10)   C / D

11)   A / B

12)   C / D

13)   A / B

14)   C / D

15)   A / B

16)   C / D

Follow and scan the QR code to view the tutorial video on this topic.
Sigue y escanea el código QR para ver el video tutorial sobre este tema.

- **EXERCISE #5: The following vocabulary words have the /ph/ digraph sound at the beginning of the word.**

Look at the words on the list below and practice pronouncing each word. (Use the QR to assist you in discriminating the initial /ph/ sound in each word)

Word Bank

pharmacist (n) \fär ma sist\    phantom (n) \fan tem\

phoneme (n) \fō nēm\   physics (n) \fi ziks\

phobia (n) \fō bē a\    phase (n) \fāz\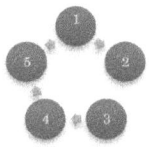

physician (n) \fe zi shen\    pharmacy (n) \fär ma sē\

photocopy (n) \fō tō kă pē\    photographer (n) \fō tō graf er\

phrase (n) \frāz\   *"Raining Cats & Dog*   photo (n) \fōtō\

- **EXERCISE #6: Discriminating the /ph/ sound at the beginning of a word.**

    Look at each set of pictures, listen to each word, and then circle the correct picture that makes the /ph/ digraph sound. (Use the QR to assist you in this next exercise)

1)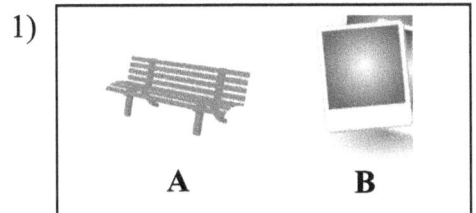

2)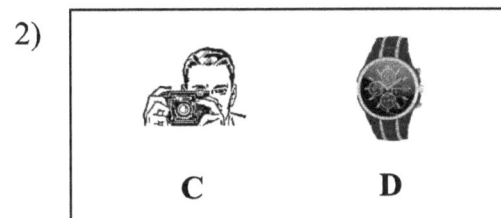

3)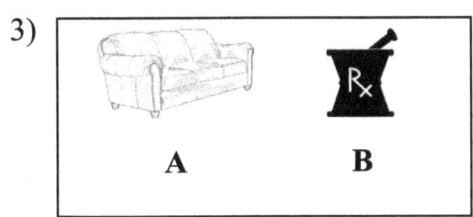

4)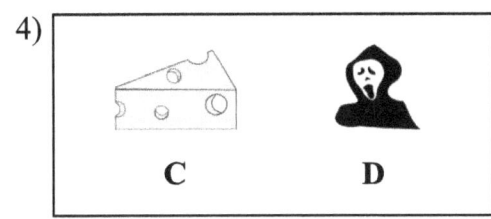

5)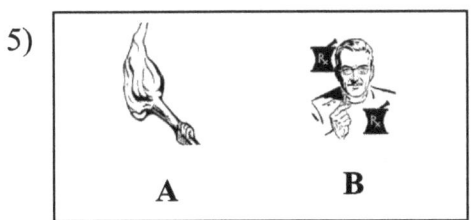

6)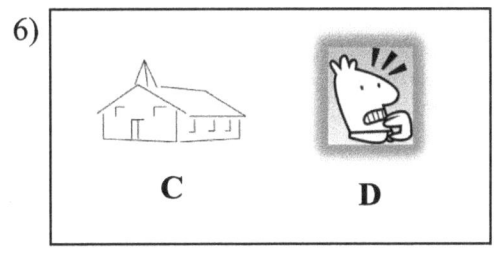

7)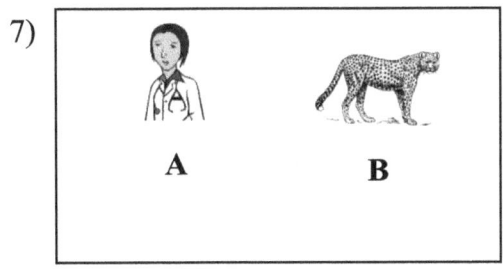

8)

Follow and scan the QR code to view the tutorial video on this topic.
Sigue y escanea el código QR para ver el video tutorial sobre este tema.

- **EXERCISE #7**: In this exercise, you will listen to each of the words below and repeat its pronunciation emphasizing the /ph/ digraph sound. Then you will underline the /ph/ consonant digraph. (Use the QR to assist you in discriminating the initial /ph/ sound in each word)

pharmacist	phantom	phoneme	physics
phobia	phase	physician	pharmacy
photocopy	photograph	phrase	photo

Follow and scan the QR code to view the tutorial video on this topic.
Sigue y escanea el código QR para ver el video tutorial sobre este tema.

- **EXERCISE #8:** In this exercise, you will hear certain words from previous exercises and repeat them. Then, write the word you hear and say on each of the lines below.

1) _____   2) _____   3) _____
4) _____   5) _____   6) _____
7) _____   8) _____   9) _____

Follow and scan the QR code to view the tutorial video on this topic.
Sigue y escanea el código QR para ver el video tutorial sobre este tema.

NOTES:
_____
_____
_____

- **EXERCISE #9: The following words have the /ph/ digraph and the single sound is found in the middle and end of a word.**

Word Bank

alphabet (n) \ăl fă bêt \

asphalt (n) \ăs fault\

autograph (n) \ă tō grăf \

atmosphere (n) \ăt mŏs fēr\

dolphin (n) \dŏl fin\

catastrophe (n) \kă tăs trō fē\

apostrophe (n) \ă pŏs trō fē\

elephant (n) \êl ŏ fănt\

graph (n) \grăf\

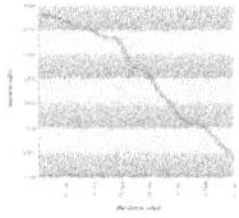

graphic (n) \ grăf ĭc\

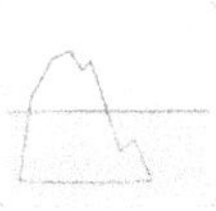

gopher (n) \gō fêr\

geography (n) \gē ŏ gră fē\

nephew (n) \ne fēū\

orphan (n) \ōr făn\

telephone (n) \te le fōn\

sphere (n) \ sfēr\

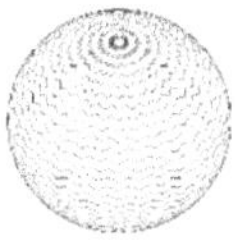

Follow and scan the QR code to view the tutorial video on this topic.
Sigue y escanea el código QR para ver el video tutorial sobre este tema.

- **EXERCISE #10: Discriminating the /ph/ sound at the beginning, middle, and end of a word.**

    Look at each set of pictures, listen to each word, and then circle the correct picture that makes the /ph/ digraph sound. (Use the QR to assist you in this next exercise)

1)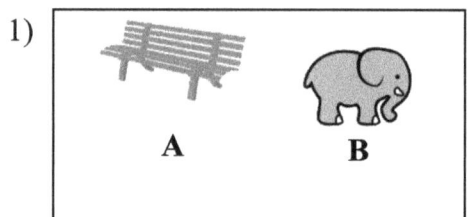

2)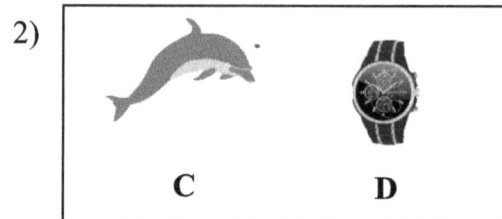

3)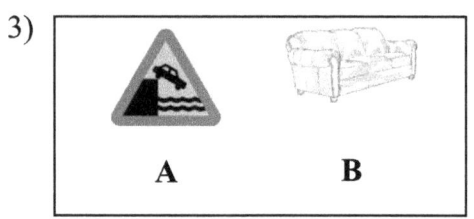

4)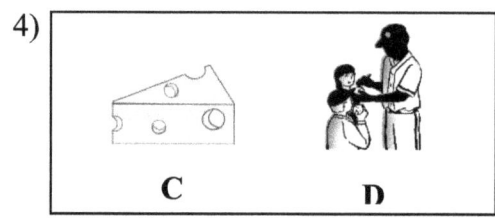

5)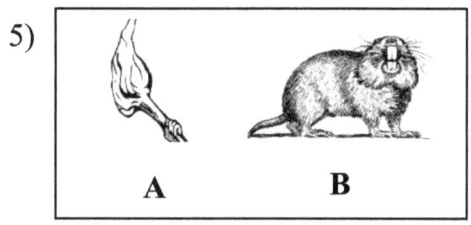

6)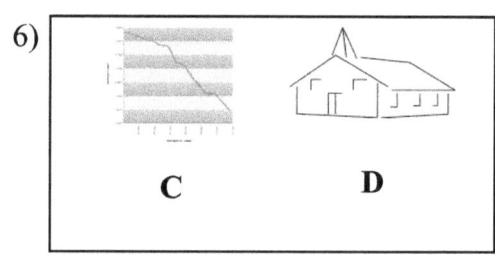

7)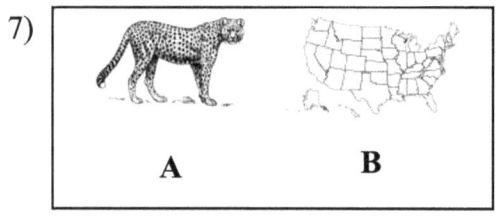

8)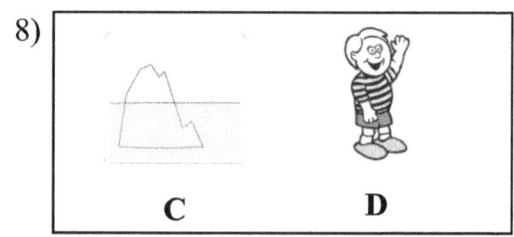

9)

10)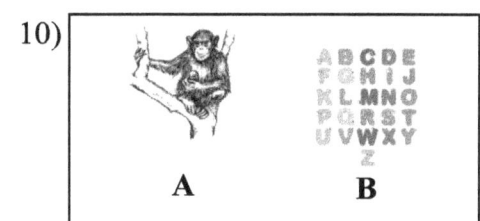

11)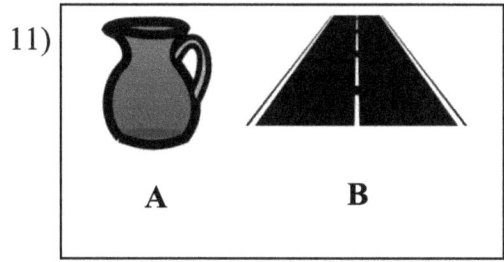

12)

13)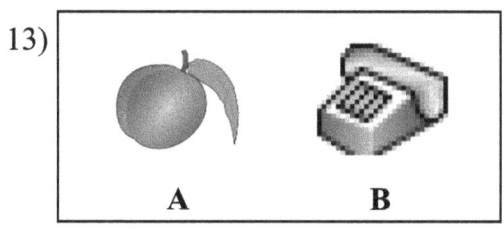

14)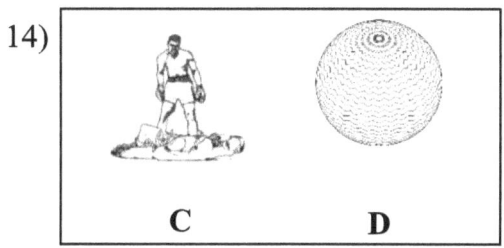

15)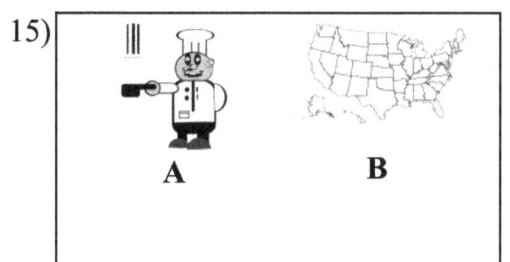

16)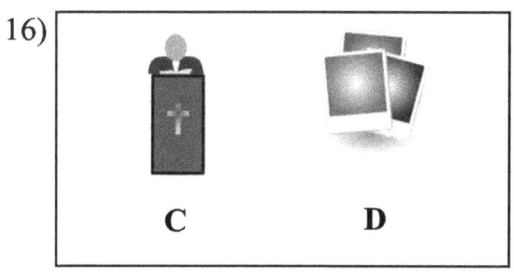

Steps to Success Digraph

➢ **Check for Understanding:**

1. In your own words, explain how digraphs are made up _____
_____

2. A digraph can be found in _____, _____, and _____ of a word.

3. Write the words from the word bank that have /ph/ digraph in the middle and end of the word.

apostrophe   phantom   elephant   a) _____   b) _____

photo   graph   physics   c) _____   d) _____

gopher   phrase   dolphin   e) _____

NOTES:

_____
_____
_____
_____
_____
_____
_____
_____
_____

Cesar Carrasco, M.Ed.

MORE DIGRAPHS

th = /th/	**sh = /sh/**	**wh = /wh/**
kn = /kn/	**gh = /gh/**	**ng = /ng/**

- Other digraphs such as /th/, /sh/, /wh/, /kn/, /gh/, and /ng/ are also digraphs made up of two letters in a word that make a single sound when combined together.

- These combined sounds known as digraphs can also be found either in the beginning, middle, or end of a word.

- The purpose of working with digraph sounds is to:
  - Understand that two letters work together to make a single sound.

  - As a second language learner, it is important to sound out the given vocabulary in this volume's exercises and emphasize the digraph you are working with to strengthen your pronunciation skills.
  -
  - As a second language learner, it is also critical that you practice the initial sounds of letters of the alphabet to discriminate the consonant patterns and blends of a word. Practicing this skill will help you understand that a single sound is heard differently than when you place two consonants together, known as a digraph.

  (Use the QR to assist you in practicing the initial sounds of the alphabet)

✓ As you work on the following exercises, not only should you emphasize the consonant digraph in each word by repeating the vocabulary word, you should also make a mental note of where the digraph lies. Understanding that the digraph lies either at the beginning, middle, or end of a word will assist you in pronouncing the word correctly but also give you a better understanding of the meaning of the word.

Steps to Success Digraph

Let's Practice!

- **EXERCISE #11: Practice saying the following vocabulary words with the /th/ digraph.** (To assist you with discriminating the /th/ digraph sound found in the beginning, middle, or end of the word, use the QR)

Word Bank

thumb (n) \th ŭ m\   thick (adj) \th ĭ k\

three (n) \th r ē\   thermometer (n) \th r mo meter\

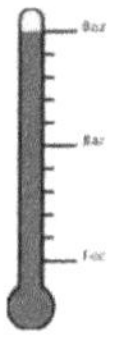

thirsty (adj) \thrs stē\   thousand (n) \th ous and\   1,000

thorn (n) \th ōrn\   throat (n) \thr ōt\

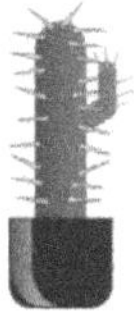

thirteen (n) \thr tēn\   thread (n) \thr ed\

Follow and scan the QR code to view the tutorial video on this topic.
Sigue y escanea el código QR para ver el video tutorial sobre este tema.

wealth (n) \welth\

athlete (n) \ath let\

cathedral (n) \că thē drŭl\

father (n) \f ŏ th r\

mother (n) \m ŏ th r\

brother (n) \brŏ th r\

bath (n) \b ă th\

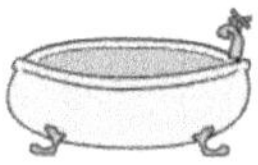

month (n) \m ŏ n th\

authentic (adj) \ă ŭ th ên tĭc\   "Rolex"

broth (n) \br ŏ th\

Thursday (n) \th r s dā\

thought (n) \thot\

- **EXERCISE #12: Discriminating the /th/ sound at the beginning, middle, and end of a word.** Look at each set of pictures, listen to each word, and then circle the picture that makes the /th/ digraph sound. (Use the QR to assist you in this next exercise)

1)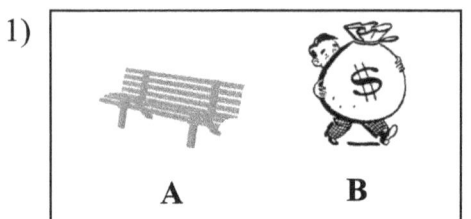

2)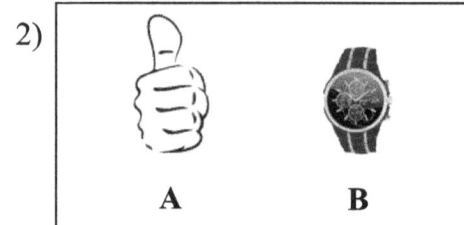

3)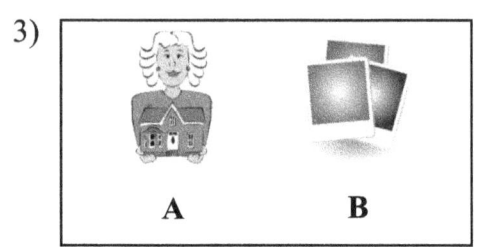

4)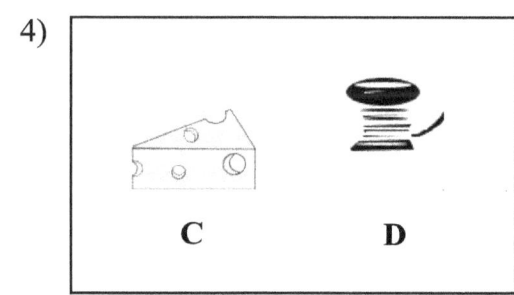

5)

6)

7)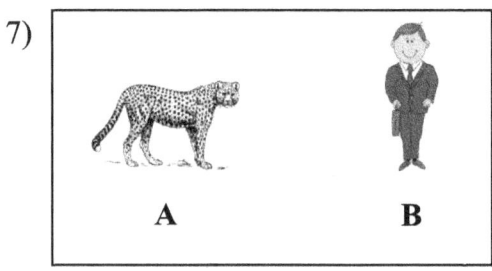

8)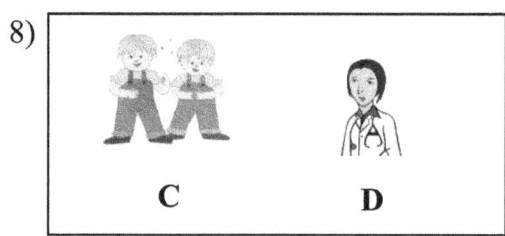

Follow and scan the QR code to view the tutorial video on this topic.
Sigue y escanea el código QR para ver el video tutorial sobre este tema.

9)

10)

11)

12)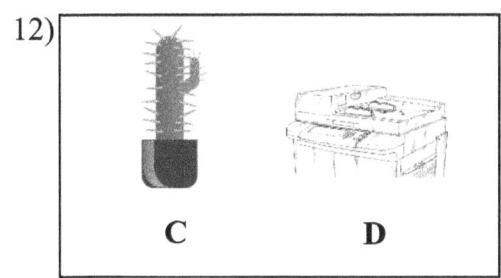

13)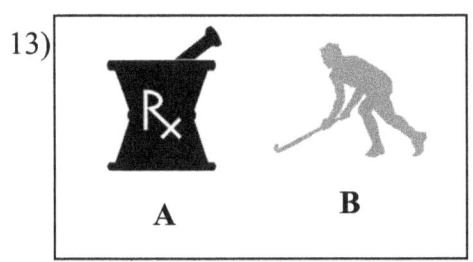

14)

15)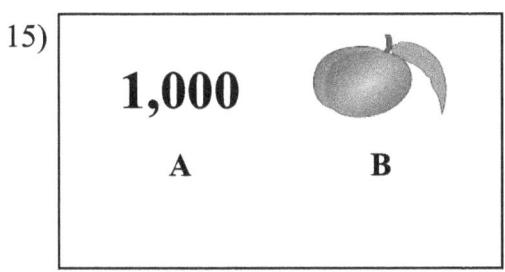

16)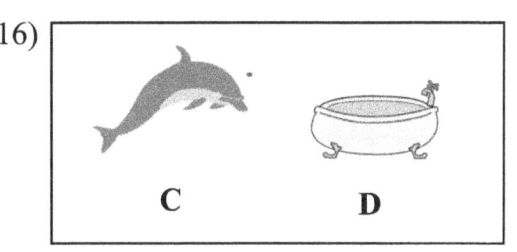

Follow and scan the QR code to view the tutorial video on this topic.
Sigue y escanea el código QR para ver el video tutorial sobre este tema.

- **EXERCISE #13: Practice saying the following vocabulary words with the /sh/digraph.**

(You may use the QR to assist you in practicing to discriminate the /sh/ digraph sound found at the beginning, middle, or end of the word)

Word Bank

shampoo (n) \sham pu\

shower (n) \shŏ wr\

shingles (n) \sh êen gls\

shoes (n) \sh ūz\

shrub (n) \shr ŭb\

shackles (n) \sh ă kls\

show (n) \sh ō\

bashful (adj) \b ă sh fŭl\

marshmallow (n) \ mar sh mêlō\

washer (n) \wă sh r\

shop (n) \sh ŏp\

trash (n) \tră sh\

shell (n) \shêl\

crash (n) \cr ă sh\

28

ship (n) \sh ĭp\

brush (n) \br ŭ sh\

mother (n) \m ŏ th r\

brother (n) \brŏ th r\

bush (n) \b ŭ sh\

dish (n) \d ĭ sh\

sheet (n) \sh ē t\

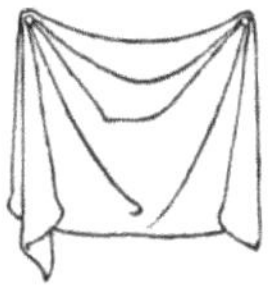

shin guards (n) \shin gărds\

shake (n) \sh āk\

shabby (adj) \sh ă bē\

hash browns (n) \jăsh brŏwns\

shut (v) \shŭt\

fresh (adj) \ fr e sh\

shallow (adj)\ sh ă lo\

Follow and scan the QR code to view the tutorial video on this topic.
Sigue y escanea el código QR para ver el video tutorial sobre este tema.

Steps to Success Digraph

- **EXERCISE #14: Discriminating the /sh/ sound at the beginning, middle, and end of a word.**

   Look at each set of pictures, listen to each word, and then circle the picture that makes the /sh/ digraph sound. (Use the QR to assist you in this next exercise)

1)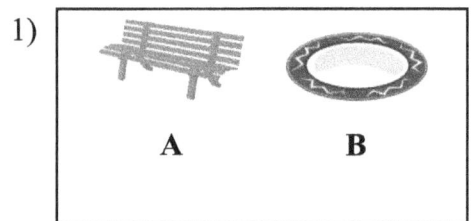

2)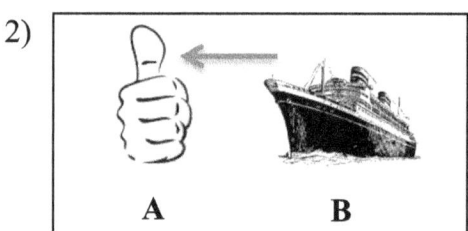

3)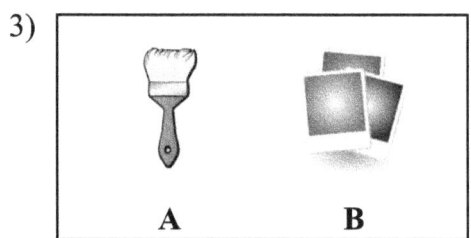

4)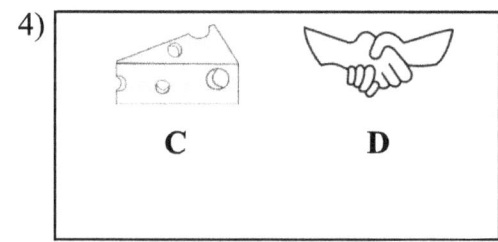

5)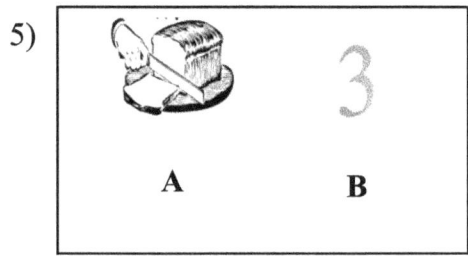

6)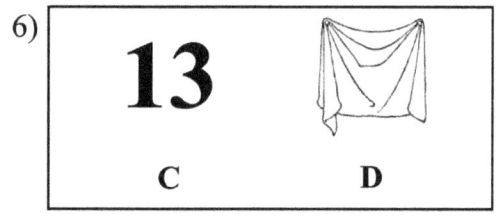

7)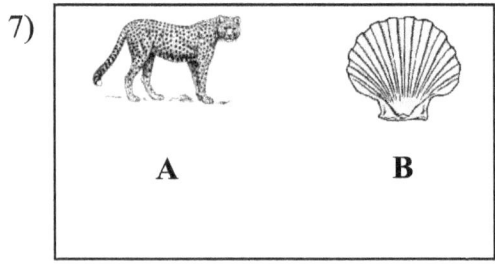

8)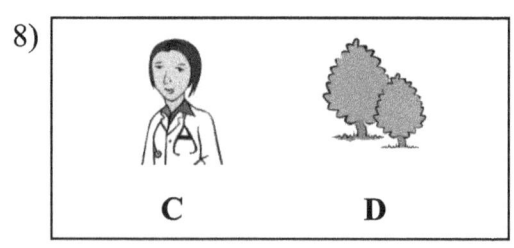

9)

A   B

10)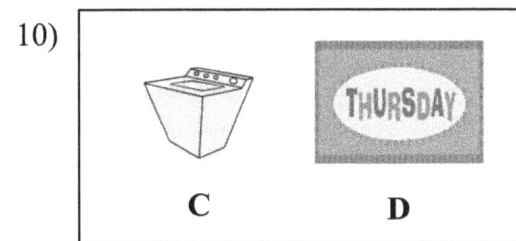

C   D

11)

A   B

12)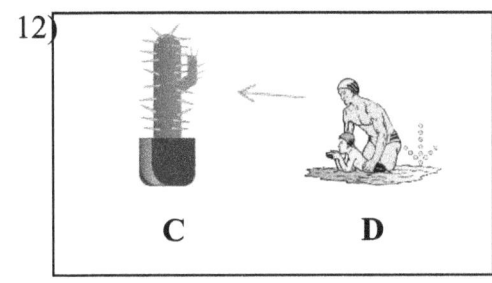

C   D

13)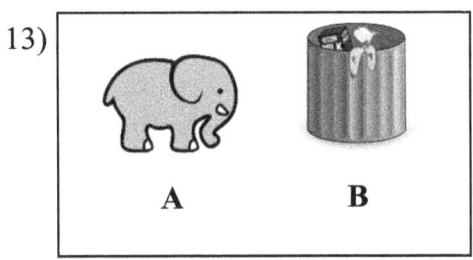

A   B

14)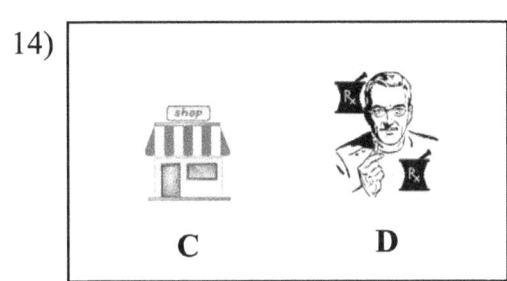

C   D

15)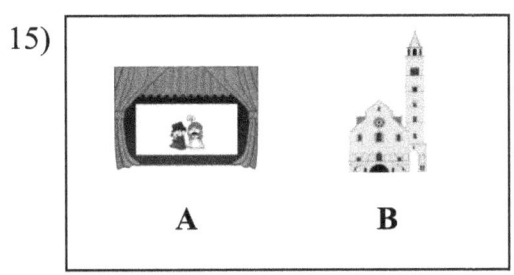

A   B

16)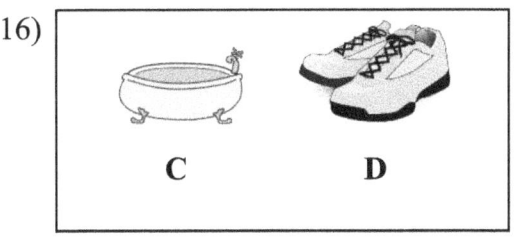

C   D

Follow and scan the QR code to view the tutorial video on this topic.
Sigue y escanea el código QR para ver el video tutorial sobre este tema.

Steps to Success Digraph

- **EXERCISE #15:** Look at the words on the list below and practice pronouncing each word with the /kn/ digraph. (You may use the QR to assist you in practicing to discriminate the /kn/ digraph sound found at the beginning, middle, or end of the word)

Work Bank

1) acknowledge (n) \ăk nŏ lêch\

2) knight (n) \n ī t\

3) knife (n)\ n ī f\

4) knee (n) \nē\

5) knew (adj) \nū\

6) knob (n) \nŏb\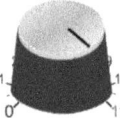

7) knock (n) \nŏk\

8) knot (n) \nŏt\

9) knockout (n) \nŏk ŏūt\

10) known (n) \nōwn\

11) knuckle (n) \ nŭk ōl\

12) kneel (v) \nēl\

13) knit (n) \nĭt\

14) unknown (adj) \ ŭn nōwn\

Follow and scan the QR code to view the tutorial video on this topic.
Sigue y escanea el código QR para ver el video tutorial sobre este tema.

- **EXERCISE #16: Discriminating the /kn/ sound at the beginning, middle, and end of a word.**

Look at each set of pictures, listen to each word, and then circle the correct picture that makes the /**kn**/ digraph sound. (Use the QR to assist you in this next exercise)

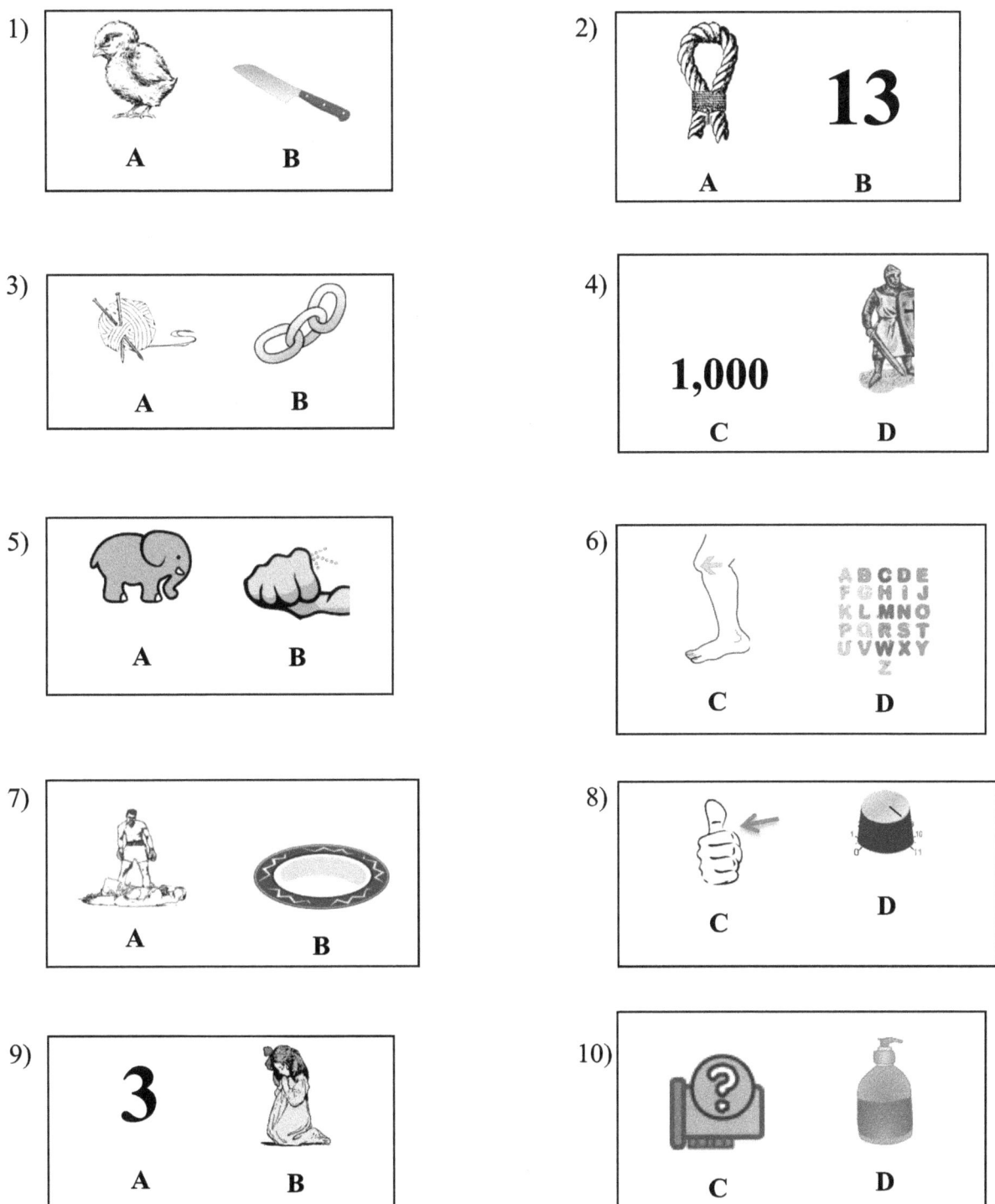

Follow and scan the QR code to view the tutorial video on this topic.
Sigue y escanea el código QR para ver el video tutorial sobre este tema.

Sharpening Your Writing Skills!

Objectives:

- Students will be able to practice reading and writing words with consonant digraphs /ch/ and /ph/.

- Students will be able to follow certain patterns so they may ask and answer informational questions with "what?"

➢ Throughout this section, you will have an opportunity to continue practicing writing informational questions with "**what**?" using already learned vocabulary words with the /**ch**/ and /**ph**/ digraphs.

➢ To assist you in being successful in writing basic informational questions with "**what**" using the /ch/ and /ph/ digraphs, follow these next rules:

 The word "**what**" is an informational question?

 An informational question with "**what**" asks about a thing.

 Informational questions with "**what**" are accompanied by the following helping verbs:

Table A

	Verb To Be	
Pronouns	**Present Progressive**	**Past**
I	am	was
he, she, it	is	was
they, you, we	are	were

Table B

	Helping Verbs		
Pronouns	**Present**	**Past**	**Future**
I	do	did	will
he, she, it	does	did	will
they, you, we	do	did	will

> 💡 **Rule to Remember:** A digraph is made up two consonants and together the two make <u>one sound.</u>

✦ It is important to be aware and understand that when writing basic informational questions with **"what,"** you can write sentences asking questions **with** or **without** action. A question asking about what an object or subject is doing, will do, or did, must have a statement that asserts what the object or subject is doing.

✦ In the next exercises, you will be writing basic sentences by asking and answering informational questions with **"what."** Follow the pattern below to help you learn the routine of forming and answering informational questions with **"what."**

Pattern:

   Question: <u>Question Word (what)</u> + <u>Helping Verb</u> + <u>Subject</u> + <u>Main Verb</u> ?

   Answer: <u>Noun/Pronoun</u> + <u>Main Verb</u> + <u>Vocabulary Word (noun)</u>.

Steps to Success Digraph

- **Exercise #17:** Use the verb and pronoun on the left-hand side to write an informational question with "what." Then, use the noun that has the /ch/ digraph sound found on the left-hand side column to answer each question. The first one is done for you.

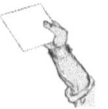

1. **Progressive**

    (wear, he)   <u>What</u>   <u>is</u>   <u>he</u>   <u>wearing</u> ?
              question word   helping verb   pronoun   verb

    (watch)   He   is wearing   a watch .
              pronoun   verb (progressive)   object

    > **Note:** Although the verb in parenthesis is written in the present tense, the question is asking in the progressive tense—right now. Therefore, when forming a question in the present participle/progressive tense, either "am," "is," or "are" is used to indicate that an –ing needs to be added to the base word to form the progressive tense.

2. **Future**

    (eat, we) _____   _____   _____ _____ ?
              question word   helping verb (future)   pronoun   verb

    (peach)   _____   _____   _____ .
              pronoun   verb (future)   object (plural)

    Follow and scan the QR code to view the tutorial video on this topic.
    Sigue y escanea el código QR para ver el video tutorial sobre este tema.

3. **Future**

    (paint, she) _____   _____ _____ _____ ?
                    question word   helping verb (future) pronoun verb (present)

    (bench) _____   _____   _____ .
             pronoun   verb (future)   object (noun)

Hint: When one is asking a question in the Future Tense, the question can have the word "will" as the helping verb and when one answers the question, we must use the present tense verb, for example: "will + present tense verb."

---

4. **Progressive**

    (make, she) _____   _____   _____   _____ ?
                question word helping verb (progressive) subject verb

    (sandwich) _____   _____   _____ .
               subject   verb (progressive)   vocabulary word (noun)

Steps to Success Digraph

5. **Progressive**

(hold, I) _____ _____ _____ _____ ?
              question word   helping verb   subject   verb (progressive)

(lunch bag) _____ _____ _____ .
                subject   verb (progressive)   object (noun)

6. **Progressive**

(write, he) _____ _____ _____ _____ ?
            question word helping verb pronoun/subject verb (progressive)

(check) _____ _____ _____ .
         subject   verb (progressive)   object (noun)

Hint: Although the verb is written in the present tense, the question asks about an action that is taking place at that moment. Therefore, you need to look at the pronoun and match it with the correct helping verb. (See Table A on Page 34)

7. **Past**

(hold, he) _____ _____ _____ _____ ?
          question word helping verb subject verb (present)

(torch) _____ _____ _____ .
       pronoun/subject irregular verb (past) object (noun)

> Hint: The question is asking you to write the sentence in the past tense, therefore, the helping verb needs to be written in the past tense and the verb in the question remains in the present tense. Also, when you answer the question, the verb needs to be written in the past tense. (See Table B on Page 35)
>
> When answering the question, the helping verb can guide you on whether the verb needs to be written in the present, past, future, or in the present participle.

- **Exercise # 18:** Using the verb and pronoun on the left-hand side, you will write an informational question with "**what**." Then, you will use the noun that has the /**ph**/ digraph sound found on the left-hand column to answer each question.

1. Progressive (pharmacist, do)

    Q: <u>What</u> _____ _____ _____ _____ ?
        question word   helping verb   subject   verb (progressive)

    (pharmacist, fill, prescription)

    A: _____ _____ _____ _____ .
        noun (subject)   helping verb   verb (progressive)   noun (object)

2. Progressive (phantom, do)

    Q: _____ _____ _____ _____ ?
        question word   helping verb   subject   verb (progressive)

    (phantom, fly)

    A: _____ _____ _____ .
        noun (object)   helping verb   verb (progressive)

Steps to Success Digraph

3. Future (physician, practice)

   Q: _____ _____ _____ _____?
         question word   helping verb   subject   verb

   (physician, practice, medicine)

   A: _____ _____ _____ _____.
         noun (subject)   helping verb   verb   noun

4. Past (photographer, take)

   Q: What _____ _____ _____?
         question word   helping verb   subject   verb (present)

   (photographer, take, photos)

   A: _____ _____ _____.
         noun (subject)   verb (past tense)   noun (object)

5. Progressive (man, copy)

   Q: What _____ _____ _____?
         question word   helping verb   subject   verb (progressive)

   (man, copy, document)

   A: _____ _____ _____ _____.
         noun (subject)   helping verb   verb (progressive)   noun (object)

Follow and scan the QR code to view the tutorial video on this topic.
Sigue y escanea el código QR para ver el video tutorial sobre este tema.

6. Progressive   (boy, do)

Q: <u>What</u> _____ _____ _____ ?
    question word   helping verb   subject   verb (progressive)

(boy, knock, on, door)

A: _____ _____ _____ _____ _____ .
   noun (subject) helping verb verb (progressive) preposition noun (object)

NOTES:

Reforzando Nuestras Habilidades de Escritura

Objetivos:

- Los estudiantes van a poder practicar leyendo e escribiendo palabras que tienen dígrafos con la /ch/ y /ph/.
- Los estudiantes van a poder seguir ciertos patrones para poder preguntar y contestar preguntas de información con **"what"** (que) usando vocabulario que tienen los dígrafos /ch/ y /ph/.

> Atreves de esta sección, tendrás la oportunidad de continuar practicando escribiendo preguntas de información con **"what"** (que) usando vocabulario que has estado escuchando y repitiendo con los dígrafos /ch/ y /ph/.

> Para asistirte en tener excito escribiendo preguntas de información básicas con **"what"** (que) y los dígrafos /ch/y /ph/, sigue estas reglas:

> > La palabra **"what"** (que) es una pregunta informativa.
> > Una pregunta informativa con **"what"** pregunta sobre una cosa.

> > Las preguntas básicas con **"what"** son acompañadas por los siguientes verbos auxiliares que se encuentran en la anterior pagina 30.

Hay que estar consientes de que las preguntas de información con **"what"** (que) se pueden escribir con palabras de acción o sin palabras de acción (verbos).

Preguntas básicas que muestran acción sobre de un sujeto o un objeto sobre lo que está haciendo, va hacer, o lo que hizo, se tiene que escribir una declaración usando una palabra de acción o lo que se le llama un "verbo."

> En estos siguientes ejercicios, escribirás oraciones básicas preguntando y contestando preguntas de información con **"what."**
> Los patrones de como preguntar y contestar que están en la pagina anterior te ayudaran a aprender la rutina de formar oraciones básicas para preguntar y contestar preguntas de información.
> También es importante aparte de escribir oraciones para preguntar y contestar preguntas de información con **"what,"** practicar diciendo la pregunta y respuesta usando el QR. Este tipo de practica te ayudara a fortalecer tu pronunciación del vocabulario, a pronunciar vocabulario con fluidez, y a desarrollar la habilidad de conversar con otros.

Cesar Carrasco, M.Ed.

Making Statements With "Where"

Objectives:

- Students will be able to practice reading and writing words with consonant digraphs /**sh**/ and /**wh**/.

- Students will be able to follow certain patterns so they may ask and answer informational questions with "**where**" using vocabulary that has /**sh**/ and /**wh**/ digraphs.

➢ **In this next exercise, you will practice writing informational questions with "where" using vocabulary words that have the consonant sounds /sh/ and /wh/.**

To continue supporting you in being successful when writing basic informational questions with "**where**," review these next set of rules which are part of *Steps to Success: A GUIDE TO BASIC GRAMMAR SKILLS*.

 Informational questions with "**where**" are accompanied by the following helping verbs: **am, is, are, do, does, was, were, did**, and **will.**

(Refer to Table A and Table B if needed on page 34 and 35)

 Some questions with "**where**" are used with **Non-action Verbs** known as Linking Verbs. Other questions with "**where**" are used with the main verb known as **Action Verbs.**

 Informational questions with "**where**" are accompanied by a preposition. Prepositions are used with nouns or pronouns to show time, the location of a person or a thing, also known as **Object of the Preposition.**

 An "**Object of the Preposition**" follows a preposition. The Object of the Preposition is the subject or object to which the answer of the informational question refers to.

The following tables show the most common prepositions when referring to a location and time:

Table C — Prepositions of Location

above	sobre	behind	detrás	with	con
after	después	beneath	debajo	without	sin
among	entre	below	abajo	over	encima
against	contra	between	entre	outside	fuera de
along	junto con, a lo largo	beyond	mas allá de	far from	lejos de
across	a lo ancho	before	antes	far away	lejos de
about	aproximado	except	excepto	during	durante
around	alrededor de	under	debajo de	since	desde
at	en	on top of	arriba de	through	atraves de
down	abajo	near	cerca	next to	en seguida de
up	arriba	into	dentro de	until	hasta que
in front of	delante de, enfrente de	on	sobre	inside	dentro
in back of	detrás	in the back of	atrás de	beside	a un lado de

Table D

Prepositions of Time

at	a las, en
on	en
in	dentro

Table E

Prepositions of Destination

toward	hacia	**of**	de
to	a	**for**	para
from	de	**by**	junto a, cerca de

- Our first skill is to practice writing informational questions with **"where"** that do not show action. Here are some guidelines to remember when you write or say informational questions with **"where:"**

  - Helping Verbs such as **"is," "are,"** and **"am,"** are Linking Verbs that do not show action.

  - A Linking Verb describes a subject or object of a sentence.

  - A question with **"where"** that is accompanied by a Linking Verb such as **"am," "is,"** or **"are,"** asks you to describe the subject or object of its location without the phrase stating action.

  - The pattern to form an informational question with **"where"** that does not show action is the following:

    > **Question Word (where) + Helping Verb + Noun?**

  - To answer **"where"** questions that do not show action—follow the next pattern to facilitate your progress:

    > **Noun + Helping Verb + Preposition + Object of the Preposition.**

NOTES:

_____
_____
_____
_____
_____
_____
_____

Objetivos:

- Los estudiantes van a poder practicar leyendo e escribiendo palabras que tienen dígrafos con la /sh/ y /wh/.

- Los estudiantes van a poder seguir ciertos patrones para poder preguntar y contestar preguntas de información con "**where**" (donde) usando vocabulario que tienen los dígrafos /sh/ y /wh/.

➢ En esta siguiente sección practicaras escribiendo preguntas de información con "**where**" (donde) usando vocabulario con las consonantes /sh/ y /wh/ que cuando las repites, ambas hacen un sonido singular.

➢ Las preguntas informativas con "**where**" son acompañadas de un verbo auxiliar: am, is, are, do, does, and will.

➢ Algunas preguntas con "**where**" *(donde)* son usadas con verbos que no muestran acción conocidos como verbos de conexión. Otras preguntas con "**where**" son usadas con el verbo principal conocidos como verbos de acción.

➢ Un objeto de la preposición (Object of the Preposition) es seguido por una preposición. El objeto de la preposición es la cosa a la que se refiere la frase.

➢ Las tablas de preposiciones son las mas comunes cuando quieres referirte a la localidad de un lugar, persona, o cosa.

❖ Nuestra primer tarea para esta sección es practicar escribiendo preguntas de información con "**where**" que no muestran acción. Las siguientes son guías para ayudarte a escribir o decir preguntas de información con "**where**" (donde):

   ✓ Verbos Auxiliares como "is," "are," y "am," son verbos cual conexión no muestra acción.
   ✓ Un verbo auxiliar describe un sujeto o objeto de la oración.
   ✓ Una pregunta con "**where**" que es acompañada con un verbo auxiliar, hace una pregunta en la cual se tiene que describir el lugar donde se encuentra el objeto o sujeto sin que la frase enseñe acción.

Cesar Carrasco, M.Ed.

Making Statements with "Where" Using

Linking Verbs and Prepositions

- **EXERCISE #19:** Use the vocabulary in the parenthesis to assist you in making an informational question with "**where**" that shows <u>no action.</u> Next, choose the best preposition found in parenthesis that will show the location of the object or subject of your question to make your answer. Finally, practice saying the question and answer

    out loud to strengthen your conversational skills.

Example:

(marshmallows)

Q: <u>**Where**</u>   <u>**are**</u>   <u>**the marshmallows**</u> ?

    Question Word   Linking Verb   Noun

(inside, on, table)

A: <u>**The marshmallows**</u>   <u>**are**</u>   <u>**on**</u>   <u>**the table**</u> .

    Noun   Linking Verb   Preposition   Object of the Preposition

> **NOTE:** The Linking Verb "are" describes the object of its location and also tells us that there is more than one marshmallow.

1. (ship)

    Q: _____   _____   _____?

        Question Word   Helping Verb   Noun

    (under, at, sea)

    A: _____ _____   _____   _____ .

        Noun   Helping Verb   Preposition   Object of the Preposition

Steps to Success Digraph

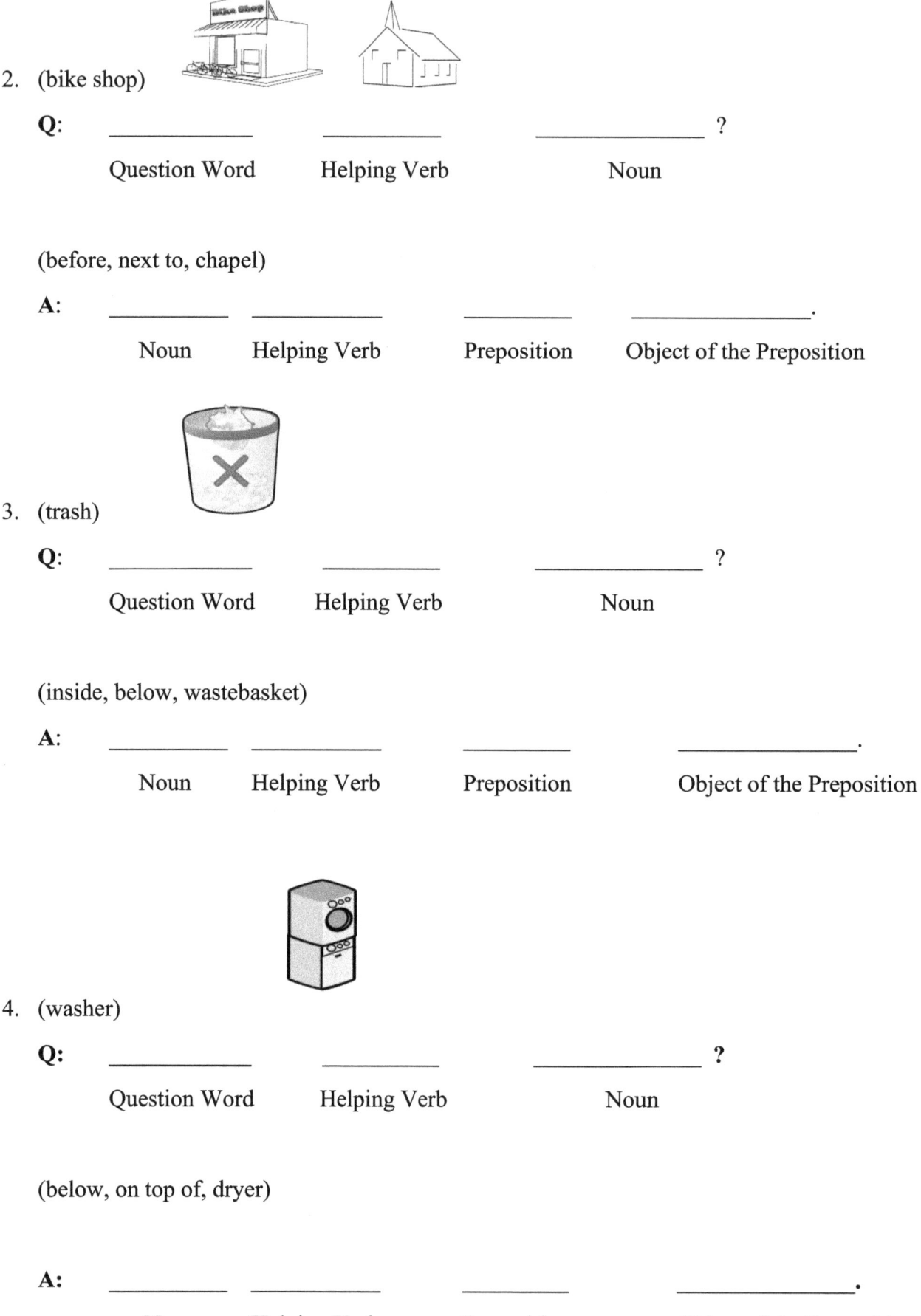

2. (bike shop)

   Q: _____ _____ _____ ?
          Question Word   Helping Verb   Noun

(before, next to, chapel)

   A: _____ _____ _____ _____.
        Noun   Helping Verb   Preposition   Object of the Preposition

3. (trash)

   Q: _____ _____ _____ ?
          Question Word   Helping Verb   Noun

(inside, below, wastebasket)

   A: _____ _____ _____ _____.
        Noun   Helping Verb   Preposition   Object of the Preposition

4. (washer)

   Q: _____ _____ _____ ?
          Question Word   Helping Verb   Noun

(below, on top of, dryer)

   A: _____ _____ _____ _____.
        Noun   Helping Verb   Preposition   Object of the Preposition

5. (shampoo)

Q: _____   _____   _____?
      Question Word   Helping Verb   Noun

(with, near, medicine bottle)

A: _____ _____   _____   _____.
    Noun Helping Verb   Preposition   Object of the Preposition

6. (toothbrush)

Q: _____   _____   _____?
      Question Word   Helping Verb   Noun

(behind, between, toothpaste and medicine bottle)

A: _____ _____   _____   _____.
    Noun Helping Verb   Preposition   Object of the Preposition

7. (sheet, hang)

Q: _____   _____   _____   _____?
      Question Word   Helping Verb   Noun   Verb (progressive)

(outside, after, patio)

A: _____ _____ _____ _____   _____.
   Noun Helping Verb Verb Preposition   Object of the Preposition

Steps to Success Digraph

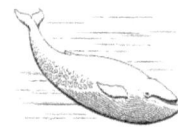

8. (whale)

Q: _____ _____ _____?
   Question Word   Helping Verb   Noun

(near, in, ocean)

A: _____ _____ _____ _____.
   Noun   Helping Verb Preposition Object of the Preposition

9. (wheelbarrow)

Q: _____ _____ _____?
   Question Word   Helping Verb   Noun

(beyond, near, bench)

A: _____ _____ _____ _____.
   Noun   Helping Verb Preposition Object of the Preposition

10. (whistle)

Q: _____ _____ _____?
   Question Word   Helping Verb   Noun

(on, behind, desk)

A: _____ _____ _____ _____.

| Noun | Helping Verb | Preposition | Object of the Preposition |

11. (wheels)

Q: _____ _____ _____ ?
        Question Word   Helping Verb   Noun

(inside, against, wall)

A: _____ _____ _____ _____ .
    Noun   Helping Verb   Preposition   Object of the Preposition

12. (shoes)

Q: _____ _____ _____ ?
        Question Word   Helping Verb   Noun

(behind, under, wheelchair)

A: _____ _____ _____ _____ .
    Noun   Helping Verb   Preposition   Object of the Preposition

Follow and scan the QR code to view the tutorial video on this topic.
Sigue y escanea el código QR para ver el video tutorial sobre este tema.

NOTES:

_____

_____

_____

Making Statements with "Where" and "What" + Action Words

1. **Objectives:**

- **Students will be able to practice reading and writing words with consonant digraphs /th/ and /kn/.**

- **Students will be able to follow certain patterns so they can ask and answer informational questions with "where" using /th/ and /kn/ digraph words that show action.**

➢ Informational questions with "**where**" showing action needs to be accompanied by a helping verb: "do," "does," "is," "am," are," or "will." (You may refer to tables A and B on page 34 and 35)

➢ The words "do" and "does" refers to the present tense. The helping verb "will" is used in the future tense.

➢ The pattern to form an informational question with "**where**" that shows action is the following:

<u>**Question Word (where) + Helping Verb + Pronoun/Noun + Verb ?**</u>

Example (a):   (shop)   Q: <u>Where do you shop?</u>

o **Notice that the question begins with "where" and asks for the location of the place where the action is taking place.**

➢ When you answer the question of "**where**," you must remember that the response needs to have a preposition followed by the object of the preposition.

➢ The pattern to answer an informational question with "**where**' is the following:

<u>**Pronoun/Noun + Verb + Preposition + Object of the Preposition.**</u>

Example (b):   (Marshalls)   A: <u>I shop at Marshalls.</u>

o **The word "at" is a prepositional word telling the person who is asking the question, *<u>the location of a place</u>*.**
o **The "Object of the Preposition" is guided by the prepositional word "at" and it refers to *<u>the location</u>*.**

Example (c): (shop)

Q: __Where__   __do__   __you__   __shop__ ?
    Question word   Helping Verb   Pronoun   Verb

A: __I__   __shop__   __at__   __Marshalls__ .
    Pronoun   Verb   Preposition   Object of the Preposition

- **Checking for Understanding**

2. Write your thoughts of what a prepositional word tells the reader.

   _____

   _____

3. Explain what the "Object of the Preposition" does in a sentence and what it precedes.

   _____

   _____

NOTES:

_____

_____

_____

_____

_____

_____

Steps to Success Digraph

Preguntas Con Donde [WHERE + ACTION WORDS] + Palabras De Acción

Objetivos:

- Los estudiantes van a poder practicar leyendo e escribiendo palabras que tienen dígrafos con /th/ y /kn/.

- Los estudiantes van a poder seguir ciertos patrones para poder preguntar y contestar preguntas de información con "**where**" (donde) usando vocabulario que tienen los dígrafos /th/ y /kn/.

➤ Preguntas informativas con "where" *(donde)* que muestran acción, necesitan estar acompañadas por un verbo auxiliar, (**do, does, is, am, are,** y **will**).

➤ Como notado en *Volumen 1, A GUIDE TO BASIC GRAMMAR SKILLS* de *"Steps to Success,"* las palabras "**do**" and" **does**" se refieren al verbo del tiempo presente. Los verbos auxiliares, "**am**," "**is**," y "**are**" se usan con el verbo progresivo. La palabra "**will**" es un verbo auxiliar que se usa en tiempo futuro.

➤ Recuerda que cuando usas un verbo de conexión "**do**," "**does**," y "**will**," estas formando una pregunta y el verbo permanece en tiempo presente.

¡Vamos a Practicar !

a) <u>Where</u>   <u>do</u>   <u>you</u>   <u>shop ?</u>   *¿Donde haces las compras?*
    QW   HV   Pron.   Verb.

b) <u>I</u>   <u>shop</u>   <u>at</u>   <u>Marshalls</u>.   *Yo hago las compras en Marshalls.*
   Pronoun   Verb   Prep.   Object of the Prep.

➤ Nota que la pregunta sigue un patrón:

Question Word + helping Verb + Pronoun + Verb.

Palabra de Pregunta + Verbo Auxiliar + Pronombre + Verbo.

➤ Recuerda que cuando una pregunta empieza con "where" (*donde*), la pregunta solamente esta preguntando por la ubicación. Por lo tanto, la respuesta termina con el objeto de la preposición.

➢ La preposición "**at**" indica a la persona que hace la pregunta la ubicación donde se lleva acabo la acción. En este caso, las compras.

NOTAS:

_____

_____

_____

_____

Let's Take Action!

- **EXERCISE#20:** Look at the word bank below and practice saying each word emphasizing the /th/ and /kn/ digraph. Next, write an informational question with "**where**" using the noun/pronoun and verb on your left-hand side. Then, answer the question using the vocabulary you see on your left-hand side. Finally, practice saying both the question and answer out loud to strengthen your conversational skills. (You may use the QR to assist you)

Word Bank

Nouns with /kn/, th/, /sh/, /ch/	Present Tense Verbs	Prepositions
theatre	go	at
ring	relax	inside
cathedral	place	outside
baths	sing	in
grandmother	take	on
knockout	like	in front of
bush	knit	under
thief	hide	knockout

Example: Present Tense (kings, go, relax)

Q: <u>Where</u>   <u>do</u>   <u>kings</u>   <u>go to relax</u> ?
   Question Word   Helping Verb   Noun   Verb

(the theatre, at)

A: <u>Kings</u>   <u>go to relax</u>   <u>at</u>   <u>the theatre</u> .
   Noun   Verb   Preposition   Object of the Preposition

Follow and scan the QR code to view the tutorial video on this topic.
Sigue y escanea el código QR para ver el video tutorial sobre este tema.

1. Past Tense   (she, place, ring)

Q: _____ _____ _____ _____ _____?
      Question Word   Helping Verb   Pronoun   Verb   Noun/Object

(inside, jewelry box)

A: _____ _____ _____ _____ _____.
      Noun   Verb   Object   Preposition   Object of the Preposition

2. Past Tense   (they, sing)

Q: _____ _____ _____ _____?
      Question Word   Linking Verb   Pronoun   Verb

(cathedral, outside)

A: _____ _____ _____ _____.
      Pronoun   Verb   Preposition   Object of the Preposition

Note: When using two verbs in the present tense, you must add "to" between the two verbs.

3. Present Tense   (birds, like, take, baths)

Q: _____ _____ _____ _____ _____
      Question Word   Helping Verb   Noun   Verb   Noun

(baths, in, fountain)

A: _____ _____ _____ _____ _____.
      Noun   Verb   Noun   Preposition   Object of the Preposition

Steps to Success Digraph

4. Present Tense   (grandmother, knit, sweater)

Q: _____ _____ _____ _____ _____?
   Question Word   Helping Verb   Noun   Verb   Noun

(on, rocking chair, sweater)

A: _____ _____ _____ _____ _____.
   Noun   Verb   Noun   Preposition   Object of the Preposition

5. Past Tense   (Joe, knockout, boxer)

Q: _____ _____ _____ _____ _____?
   Question Word   Helping Verb   Noun   Verb   Noun

(in front of, boxing gym)

A: _____ _____ _____ _____ _____.
   Noun   Verb   Noun   Preposition   Object of the Preposition

6. . Past Tense (Irregular)   (thief, hide, knife)

Q: _____ _____ _____ _____ _____?
   Question Word   Helping Verb   Noun   Verb   Noun/Object

(under, bush)

A: _____ _____ _____ _____ _____.
   Noun   Verb   Object   Preposition   Object of the Preposition

Cesar Carrasco, M.Ed.

Questions With "Why" + Action Words

- ➢ **"Why"** is used with questions when you want to find out a reason.
- ➢ A basic form to write a question for **"why"** is to follow this pattern:

<u>Why + Helping Verb (HV) + Pronoun/noun + Verb + Noun?</u>

Example: Q: <u>Why did you punch the wall ?</u>

- ➢ To answer this basic "why" question you should use this next pattern that describes your state of being using an adjective:

A: Pronoun + verb + noun + **<u>Because</u>** + <u>Pronoun/Noun + H V + Adjective.</u>

A: <u>I punched the wall because I was upset.</u>

- ➢ **Rule of Thumb:** "Because" is a conjunction word that works to join two ideas together. Sentences should not start with "**because**" when writing a sentence. However, in conversation it is common to hear sentences that start with the word "**because**."
- ➢ Adjectives describe people, places, or things. A reason to use adjectives before a noun or pronoun is to change the meaning of the sentence by making the noun or pronoun be more specific and clear.
- ➢ As stated before, whenever you are using two verbs to ask a question or to answer a question, the first verb is considered to be the main verb. The second verb being used is called the infinitive verb and it is preceded by "to." Also keep in mind that the "to" is not a preposition and the "to" is used between the two verbs to connect them, the main verb and the infinitive verb.

Noticed that "need" is the main verb and the infinitive verb, "brush" is preceded by "to."

Notes: _____

_____

_____

PREGUNTAS CON "WHY" *(porque?)*

- **Why** *(porque)* se usan en preguntas cuando quieres saber la razón.
- Una forma básica de preguntar **"why"** es siguiendo el siguiente patrón:

Why + Helping Verb + Pronoun/noun + Verb + Noun ?

Ejemplo: Q: **Why** did you punch the wall ? *¿Porque golpeaste la pared?*

Cuando contestas preguntas básicas con **"why"** debes usar el siguiente patrón para describir la razón ó el porque.

A: [I punched the wall] Because + Pronoun/Noun + Helping Verb + Adjective.

[yo golpee la pared] porque (because) + yo (I) + estaba (was) + enojado (upset).

- **Because"** es una palabra que une dos ideas juntas. También es importante de estar consiente de que al escribir una respuesta con **"why,"** no se debe de empezar con **"because."** Sin embargo, en una conversación es común escuchar la respuesta empezando con **"because."**

NOTAS:

_____

_____

_____

_____

_____.

- **EXERCISE#21:** Use the vocabulary on the left-hand side to make and answer informational questions with "**why**." Use the subject or object to help you write the correct helping verb (Use Tables A and B on Page 33 to assist you). You may make the question in the present tense, past tense, or in the present participle.

(Use may use the DVD that is included inside this book to help you strengthen your conversational skills)

1. (refuse, drink, broth, you)   (make the question in the present tense)

    Q: _____ _____ _____ _____ _____?
        Question Word   Linking Verb   Pronoun   Verb   Noun (the "what")

    (hot, broth)

    A: __Because__ _____ _____ _____.
        Conjunction   Subject/Object   Linking Verb   Adjective

2. (he, nervous)

    Q: _____ _____ _____ _____?
        Question Word   Helping Verb   Pronoun   Adjective

    (today, Friday the 13th)

    A: __Because__ _____ _____ _____.
        Conjunction   Adverb   Helping Verb   Adjective

(The word "today" is an adverb because it tells you when.)

Steps to Success Digraph

3. (look, similar, they)

   Q: _____ _____ _____ _____ _____?
         Question Word   Helping Verb   Pronoun   Verb   Adjective

   (brother)
   A: _Because___ _____ _____ _____.
         Conjunction   Pronoun   Linking Verb   Noun (plural)

4. (mother, happy)

   Q: _____ _____ _____ _____?
         Question Word   Helping Verb   Subject   Adjective

   (cook)
   A: _Because___ _____ _____ _____.
         Conjunction   Subject   Linking Verb   Verb (progressive)

5. (knight, celebrate)   (make this question in the present participle tense)

   Q: _____ _____ _____ _____?
         Question Word   Helping Verb   Subject   Verb (progressive)

   (slayed, dragon)
   A: _Because___ _____ _____ _____.
         Conjunction   Subject   Verb (past tense)   Noun

6. (he, punch, wall)   (make the question in the past tense)

    Q: _____ _____ _____ _____ _____?
          Question Word Linking Verb   Pronoun   Verb   Noun

    (upset)
    A: _ Because___ _____ _____ _____ .
         Conjunction   Pronoun   Linking Verb   Adjective   (past tense)

NOTES:

_____

_____

_____

_____

_____

_____

_____

_____

_____

_____

_____

_____

Steps to Success Digraph

- **EXERCISE# 22:** Circle the adjective in parenthesis that best describes the picture on your left hand side. Then, write the adjective on the blank space. Practice saying each sentence out loud practicing words with digraphs already learned. Follow these next rules to help you in being successful when describing each picture:

  ➢ Adjectives describe things, people, and places.
    1. Adjectives are used before the noun or pronoun.
    2. Adjectives tell us about which one, what kind, and how many.

  ➢ Adjectives are used before a noun or pronoun.

  ➢ The purpose of using adjectives before a noun or pronoun is to change the meaning of the sentence by making it specific and more direct.

  ➢ Adjectives tell us about which one, what kind, and how many.

Pattern

Q: Why +   Linking Verb + Subject/Object + Adjective

A: Because + Subject/Object + linking Verb + Adjective

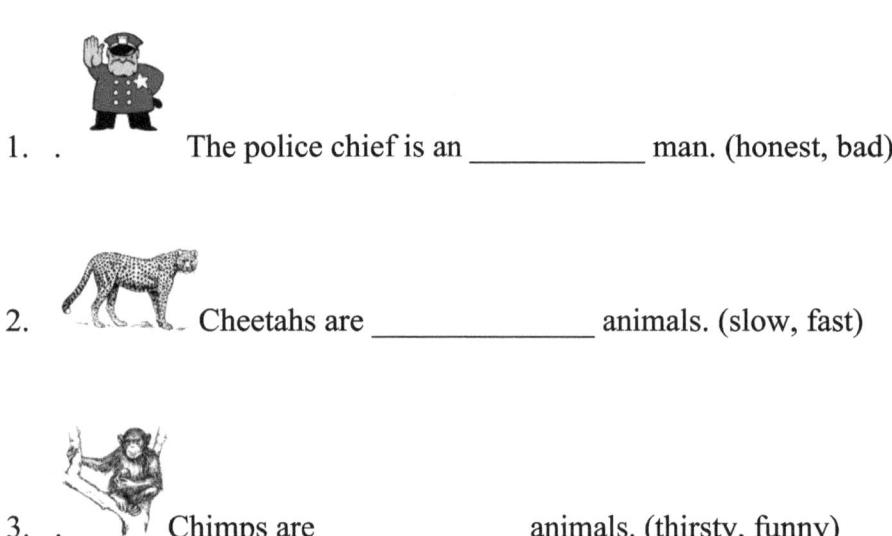

1. .   The police chief is an _____ man. (honest, bad)

2.   Cheetahs are _____ animals. (slow, fast)

3. .   Chimps are _____ animals. (thirsty, funny)

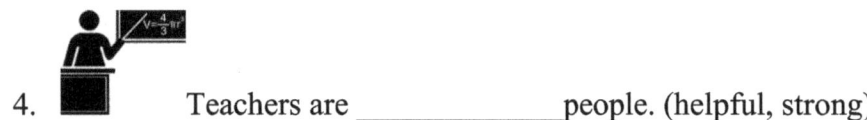

4.   Teachers are _____ people. (helpful, strong)

64

5. The _____ knife belongs to my father. (dull, sharp)

6.  The Rolex I wear is an _____ watch. (authentic, fake)

7.  A chapel is considered to be a (proud, small) building.

8.  A cathedral is a (large, tiny) building where many can fit.

9.  The chef makes _____ meals. (jealous, delicious)

10.  Mr. Brown is a _____ man. (wealthy, angry)

11.  Taylor is an (lonely, athletic) and a (tired, strong) player.

12.  The preacher is a _____ man. (kind, empty)

Follow and scan the QR code to view the tutorial video on this topic.
Sigue y escanea el código QR para ver el video tutorial sobre este tema.

Steps to Success Digraph

PREGUNTAS CON "WHY" *(porque?)*

- **Why** *(porque)* se usa en preguntas cuando quieres saber la razón.
- Una forma básica de preguntar **"why"** es siguiendo el siguiente patrón:

<u>Why</u> + <u>Helping Verb</u> + <u>Pronoun/noun</u> + <u>Verb</u> + <u>Noun</u> ?

Ejemplo: Q: <u>Why did you punch the wall</u> ? *¿Porque golpeaste la pared?*

Cuando contestas preguntas básicas con **"why"** debes usar el siguiente patrón para describir la razón ó el porque.

A: [I punched the wall] <u>Because</u> + <u>Pronoun/Noun</u> + <u>Helping Verb</u> + <u>Adjective</u>.

[yo golpee la pared] **<u>porque (because)</u>**+ <u>**yo (I)**</u> + <u>**estaba (was)**</u> + <u>**enojado (upset)**</u>

- "Because" es una palabra que une dos ideas juntas. También es importante de estar consiente de que al escribir una respuesta con **"why,"** no se debe de empezar con **"because."** <u>Sin embargo, en una conversación es común escuchar la respuesta empezando con **"because."**</u>

NOTAS:

_____
_____
_____
_____
_____
_____
_____
_____
_____

Cesar Carrasco, M.Ed.

Post-Test

1. Digraphs are combined sounds that can be found either in the beginning, middle, or end of a word.

2. In this next section, look at each picture and circle the correct digraph sound that each picture makes. Next, write the name of the picture on the blank line and then underline the word that tells whether the picture has a beginning, middle, or end digraph sound.

3. **Read each question and circle the best answer.**

   ✓ A digraph can be found in _____.

      a. the middle of a word.
      b. the beginning of a word.
      c. the beginning, middle, or end of a word.

   ✓ A digraph _____.

      a. . is made up of two letters that are combined to make a single sound.
      b. is made up of two letters to make two sounds.
      c. is made up of many letters, each making its own sound.
      d. none of the above.

4. <u>True or False</u>: **After you read each question write True or False on the blank line to justify the statement.**
   1. _____ Digraphs are two consonants that can be articulated into one sound.

   2. _____ A digraph can be found either at the beginning or end of a word.

   3. . _____ The purpose of working with digraph sounds is to understand that   two letters work together to make a single sound.

67

5. **Look at each set of pictures and circle the letter of the picture that makes the initial sound /ch/.**

    4.

        A   B

    5.

        A   B

6. **Look at each set of pictures and circle the letter of the picture that makes the /ph/ sound in the middle of a word.**

    6.

        A   B

    7.

        A   B

8.

    A   B

For questions 11 through 16, please answer questions (a), (b), and (c).

9. .

   a. The picture makes a (ch, ph, th, sh, kn, wh) digraph sound.
   b. The name of this picture is _____.
                                    Vocabulary Word

   c. **Thumb** has a (beginning, middle, end) digraph sound.
      Vocabulary Word

10. .

   a. The picture makes a (ch, ph, th, sh, kn, wh) digraph sound.
   b. The name of this picture is _____.
                                    Vocabulary Word

   c. _____ has a (beginning, middle, end) digraph sound.

     Vocabulary Word

Steps to Success Digraph

11.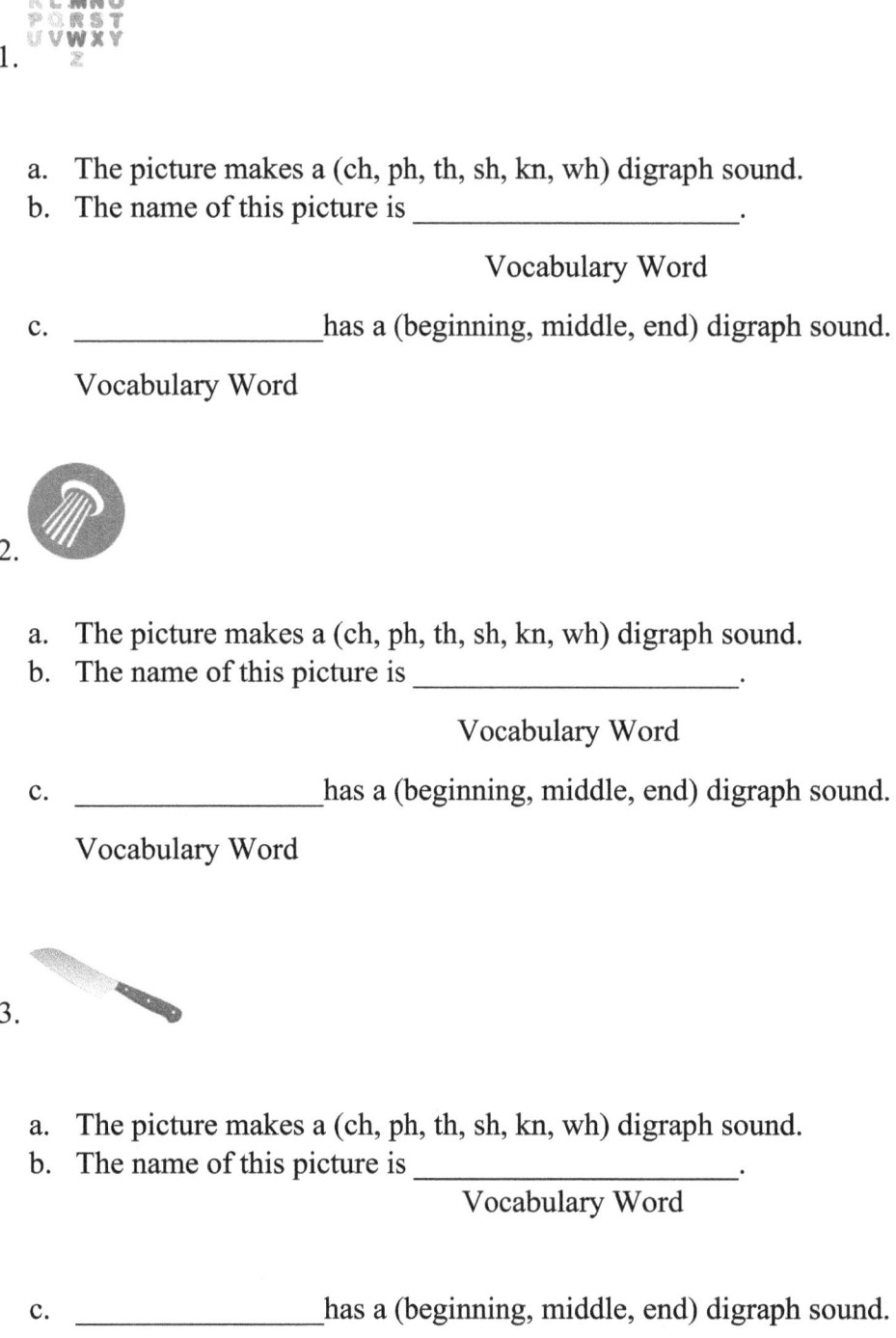

    a. The picture makes a (ch, ph, th, sh, kn, wh) digraph sound.
    b. The name of this picture is _____.
                                     Vocabulary Word

    c. _____has a (beginning, middle, end) digraph sound.

    Vocabulary Word

12.

    a. The picture makes a (ch, ph, th, sh, kn, wh) digraph sound.
    b. The name of this picture is _____.
                                     Vocabulary Word

    c. _____has a (beginning, middle, end) digraph sound.

    Vocabulary Word

13.

    a. The picture makes a (ch, ph, th, sh, kn, wh) digraph sound.
    b. The name of this picture is _____.
                                     Vocabulary Word

    c. _____has a (beginning, middle, end) digraph sound.

    Vocabulary Word

Steps to Success – DIGRAPHS

Pretest

1. c 2. a 3. T 4. T 5. T 6. A 7. B 8. A 9. B 10. B

Exercise #2:

1. A 2. D 3. B 4. C 5. A 6. D 7. A 8. D

Exercise #4:

1. A 2. D 3. B 4. C 5. A 6. D 7. A 8. D 9. A 10. C

11. B 12. D 13. A 14. C 15. A 16. D

Exercise #6:

1. B 2. C 3. B 4. D 5. B 6. D 7. A 8. D

Exercise #7:

1. <u>ph</u>armacist　　2. <u>ph</u>antom　　3. <u>ph</u>oneme　　4. <u>ph</u>ysics

5. <u>ph</u>obia　　6. <u>ph</u>ase　　7. <u>ph</u>ysician　　8. <u>ph</u>armacy

9. <u>ph</u>otocopy　　10. <u>ph</u>otograph　　11. <u>ph</u>rase　　12. <u>ph</u>oto

Steps to Success Digraph

Exercise #10:

1. B 2. C 3. A 4. D 5. B 6. C 7. B 8. C 9. B 10. D

11. B 12. D 13. B 14. D 15. B 16. D

Check for Understanding:

1. Digraphs are made up of two letters that are combined together to make a single sound.

2. In the beginning, middle, and end.

3. a) apostrophe b) elephant c) graph d) gopher e) dolphin

Cesar Carrasco, M.Ed.

Steps to Success – <u>DIGRAPHS</u>

Exercise #12:

1. B   2. C   3. A   4. D   5. B   6. C   7. B   8. C   9. B   10. D

11. B   12. C   13. B   14. C   15. A   16. D

Exercise #14:

1. B   2. D   3. A   4. D   5. A   6. D   7. B   8. D   9. B   10. C

11. B   12. D   13. B   14. C   15. A   16. D

Exercise #16:

1. B   2. C   3. A   4. D   5. B   6. C   7. A   8. D   9. B   10. C

Exercise #17:

2. Question: <u>What will we eat</u>?   Answer: <u>We will eat peaches</u>.

3. Question: <u>What is she making</u>?   Answer: <u>She is making a sandwich</u>.

4. Question: <u>What did he hold</u>?   Answer: <u>He held the torch</u>.

5. Question: <u>What am I holding</u>? Answer: <u>I am holding a lunch bag</u>.

6. Question: <u>What is he writing</u>? Answer: <u>He is writing a check</u>.

7. Question: <u>What will she paint</u>?   Answer: <u>She will paint a bench</u>.

Exercise #18:

1. Q: What is the pharmacist doing?
   A: The pharmacist is filling a prescription.

2. Q: What is the phantom doing?
   A: The phantom is flying.

3. Q: What will the physician practice?
   A: The physician will practice medicine.

4. Q: What did the photographer take?
   A: The photographer took photos.

5. Q: What is the man copying?
   A: The man is copying a document.

6. Q: What is the boy doing?
   A: The boy is knocking on a door.

Steps to Success – DIGRAPHS

Exercise #19:

1. Question: Where is the ship?   Answer: The ship is at sea.

2. Question: Where is the bike shop?   Answer: The bike shop is next to the chapel.

3. Question: Where is the trash?   Answer: The trash is inside the wastebasket.

4. Question: Where is the washer?   Answer: The washer is on top of the dryer.

5. Question: Where is the shampoo?   Answer: The shampoo is near the medicine bottle.

6. Question: Where is the toothbrush?   Answer: The toothbrush is between the toothpaste and medicine bottle.

7. Question: Where is the sheet hanging?   Answer: The sheet is hanging outside the patio.

8. Question: Where is the whale?   Answer: The whale is in the ocean.

9. Question: Where is the wheelbarrow?   Answer: The wheelbarrow is near the bench.

10. Question: Where is the whistle?   Answer: The whistle is on the desk.

11. Question: Where are the wheels?   Answer: The wheels are against the wall.

12. Question: Where are the shoes?   Answer: The shoes are behind the wheelchair.

Exercise #20:

Example: Q: Where do Kings go to relax? A: Kings go to relax at the theatre.

1. Q: Where does she place the ring?   A: She places the ring inside the jewelry box.

2. Q: Where did they sing?   A: They sang outside the cathedral.

3. Q: Where do birds take baths?   A: The birds take baths in the fountain.

4. Q: Where does grandmother knit the sweater?

   A: Grandmother knits the sweater on the rocking chair.

5. Q: Where did Joe knockout the boxer?

   A: Joe knocked out the boxer in front of the boxing gym.

6. Q: Where does the thief hide the knife?   A: The thief hid the knife under the bush.

Steps to Success – DIGRAPHS

Exercise #21:

1. Q: Why do you refuse to drink the broth?   A: Because the broth is hot.

2. Q: Why is he nervous?   A: Because today is Friday the 13th.

3. Q: Why do they look similar?   A: Because they are brothers.

4. Q: Why is mother happy?   A: Because she is cooking.

5. Q: Why is the knight celebrating?   A: Because the knight slayed the dragon.

6. Q: Why did he punch the wall?   A: Because he is upset.

Exercise #22:

1. honest   2. fast   3. funny   4. helpful   5. sharp   6. authentic

7. small   8. large   9. delicious   10. wealthy   11. athletic, strong   12. kind

Post-Test

1. c   2. a   3. T   4. T   5. T   6. A   7. B   8. A   9. B   10. A

11. a) /th/ b) thumb c) thumb, beginning   12. a) /ch/ b) torch c) torch, end

13. a) /ph/ b) alphabet c) alphabet, middle   14. a) /sh/ b) shower c) shower, beginning

15. a) /kn/ b) knife c) knife, beginning

Steps to Success Digraph

www.ingramcontent.com/pod-product-compliance
Lightning Source LLC
Chambersburg PA
CBHW042354070526
44585CB00028B/2922